THE FIRST BOOK OF NATIONAL MONUMENTS

Organ pipe cactus, Organ Pipe Cactus National Monument, Arizona
(National Park Service photo)

The FIRST BOOK of
NATIONAL MONUMENTS

by NORMAN LOBSENZ

Illustrated with photographs

FRANKLIN WATTS, INC.

575 LEXINGTON AVENUE • NEW YORK

First Printing
Library of Congress Catalog Card Number: 59-12205

© Copyright 1959 by Franklin Watts, Inc.
Printed in the United States of America

Scott's Bluff National Monument, Nebraska, a landmark on the Oregon Trail
(National Park Service photo by George Grant)

Contents

Delicate Arch, Arches National Monument, Utah (National Park Service photo)

Our National Monuments

Deep inside a Utah mountain is a cave whose walls are a rainbow of color. . . .

In the Arizona desert an amazing kind of flowering cactus grows fifty feet tall. . . .

Hidden in a rocky canyon in Colorado are the ruins of a stone tower built by prehistoric Indians over seven hundred years ago. . . .

Near Baltimore, Maryland, is an old fortress; the sight of it, with its flag still flying "in the dawn's early light," inspired the writing of our national anthem.

These sights, along with scores of others that offer thrilling scenery, weird plants and animals, and famous landmarks of United States history, are all part of every American's heritage. They are the "national monuments."

Not many Americans know them well. Although the monuments are an important part of the national park system, people in general seem to look on them as the "little brothers" of the more famous national parks.

The first national park, Yellowstone, was created by the United States Congress in 1872. But not until June, 1906, did Congress pass the act that gave the President of the United States the right

1

to establish as national monuments any "historic landmarks, historic or prehistoric structures, and other objects of scientific interest." The purpose of the act was to preserve such areas for all Americans to study and enjoy, and to prevent souvenir-hunters from ruining such spots.

In September, 1906, President Theodore Roosevelt named the first national monument. It was Devils Tower, in Wyoming. The tower is a huge column of rock formed from molten lava thrust up out of the earth millions of years ago. Its fluted pillars soar one thousand feet above the prairie, and are almost impossible to climb. The Indians' name for the tower was "Grizzly Bear's Lodge." According to their legends, a giant bear left his claw marks in the rock while trying to get to the top.

Grass and shrubs grow on the flat summit of Devils Tower, and mice and chipmunks live there. No one knows how the animals reached the height. Once a daredevil parachuter jumped from a plane to the top of the huge rock. He stayed there for six days before a National Park Service rescue group was able to get him down.

In 1933 the National Park Service in the Department of the Interior was given charge of the national monuments as well as the national parks and other historic and scenic areas of America. Actually, there is no clear-cut distinction between a national park and a national monument. The parks can be created only by an act of Congress, and they are usually large areas of magnificent scenery. Monuments can be established by Congress or by a President. They are usually smaller in size than the parks and are important for some historic or scientific reason. Two of the monuments, however, are larger than any national park. Many regions which were first set aside as national monuments have later been made national parks. (For post office addresses of the national monuments, see page 84.)

2

Devils Tower, Devils Tower National Monument, Wyoming
(National Park Service photo by George Grant)

NATIONAL MONUMENTS

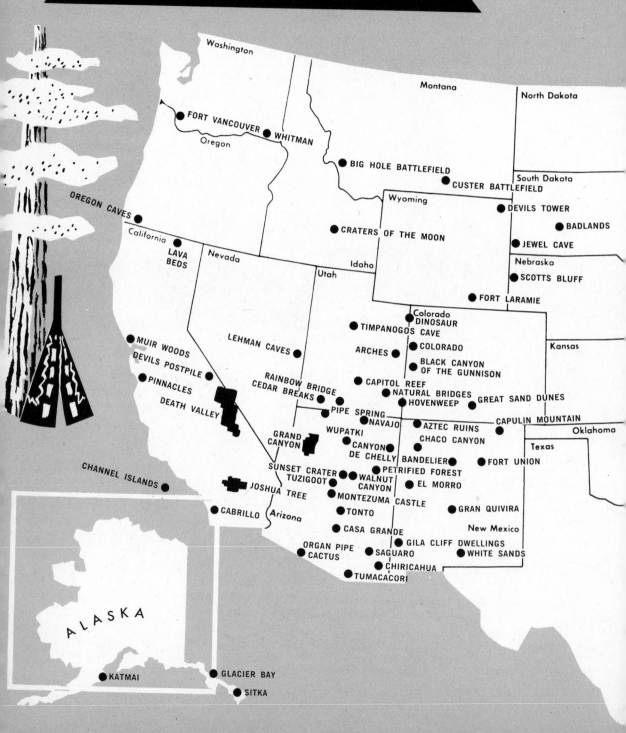

Washington

Montana

North Dakota

FORT VANCOUVER

WHITMAN

Oregon

BIG HOLE BATTLEFIELD

South Dakota

CUSTER BATTLEFIELD

Wyoming

DEVILS TOWER

OREGON CAVES

BADLANDS

California

CRATERS OF THE MOON

JEWEL CAVE

LAVA BEDS

Nevada

Nebraska

Idaho

SCOTTS BLUFF

Utah

FORT LARAMIE

Colorado

DINOSAUR

TIMPANOGOS CAVE

LEHMAN CAVES

COLORADO

MUIR WOODS

ARCHES

BLACK CANYON OF THE GUNNISON

Kansas

DEVILS POSTPILE

RAINBOW BRIDGE

CEDAR BREAKS

CAPITOL REEF

NATURAL BRIDGES

GREAT SAND DUNES

PINNACLES

HOVENWEEP

DEATH VALLEY

PIPE SPRING

CAPULIN MOUNTAIN

Oklahoma

NAVAJO

GRAND CANYON

WUPATKI

AZTEC RUINS

Texas

CHACO CANYON

CANYON DE CHELLY

BANDELIER

FORT UNION

CHANNEL ISLANDS

SUNSET CRATER

PETRIFIED FOREST

TUZIGOOT

WALNUT CANYON

EL MORRO

JOSHUA TREE

MONTEZUMA CASTLE

CABRILLO

Arizona

GRAN QUIVIRA

TONTO

CASA GRANDE

New Mexico

ORGAN PIPE CACTUS

GILA CLIFF DWELLINGS

SAGUARO

WHITE SANDS

CHIRICAHUA

TUMACACORI

ALASKA

KATMAI

GLACIER BAY

SITKA

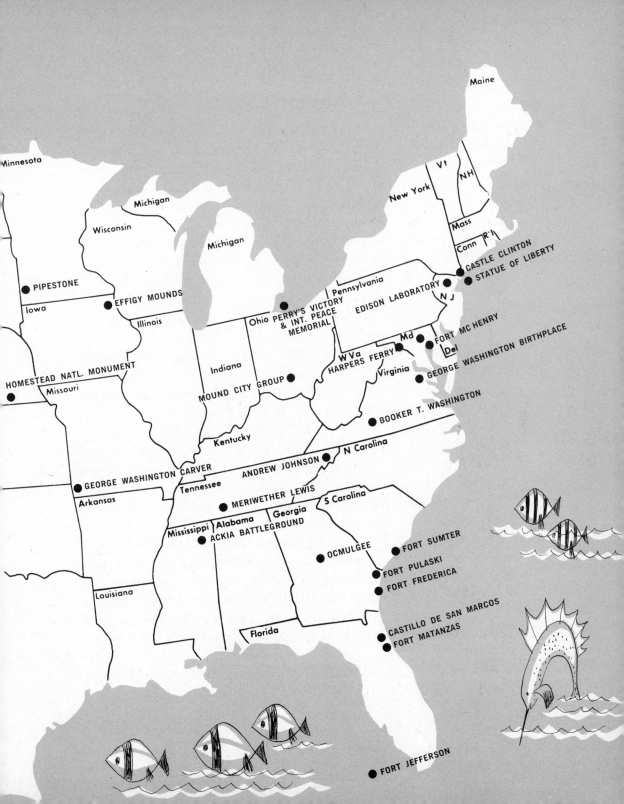

Minnesota

Michigan

Wisconsin

Michigan

Maine

Vt

New York

NH

Mass

Conn

R'I

CASTLE CLINTON

STATUE OF LIBERTY

● PIPESTONE

Iowa

● EFFIGY MOUNDS

Illinois

Ohio PERRY'S VICTORY
& INT. PEACE
MEMORIAL

Pennsylvania

EDISON LABORATORY

N J

Indiana

W Va

Md

FORT MC HENRY

Del

HARPERS FERRY

HOMESTEAD NATL. MONUMENT

MOUND CITY GROUP

Virginia

GEORGE WASHINGTON BIRTHPLACE

Missouri

Kentucky

● BOOKER T. WASHINGTON

GEORGE WASHINGTON CARVER

Tennessee

ANDREW JOHNSON

N Carolina

Arkansas

● MERIWETHER LEWIS

S Carolina

Mississippi Alabama

Georgia

● ACKIA BATTLEGROUND

● OCMULGEE

● FORT SUMTER

FORT PULASKI

FORT FREDERICA

Louisiana

CASTILLO DE SAN MARCOS

FORT MATANZAS

Florida

● FORT JEFFERSON

Prehistoric Sites

Many Americans do not realize that various Indian tribes were living in parts of North America fifteen thousand years ago, or more — long before historic times. These prehistoric tribes wandered over the continent from the far Northwest. Scientists think they first came from Asia, crossing into what is now Alaska over a bridge of land that existed in ancient times.

Wherever the prehistoric Indians lived for any length of time they left traces. Sometimes it is arrowheads or ancient stone weapons. Or it may be the ashes of an ancient campfire whose age modern scientists can detect by measuring for radioactivity. Burial mounds may be left, or the crumbling ruins of stone houses, or caves hacked out of the cliffs.

Many such prehistoric sites have been uncovered by archaeologists and explorers. The most interesting have been preserved as national monuments. They are located in three main geographic areas: the Southeast, the Midwest, and the Southwest.

In the Southeast, *Russell Cave National Monument* in Alabama is one of the few where scientists have traced man in North America back into the far, far reaches of the past. In this cave, diggers have found the ashes of an Indian campfire estimated to have given off its warmth and light nine thousand years ago. The cave is now being made ready for the public to visit.

In neighboring Georgia, *Ocmulgee National Monument* preserves the remains of earth mounds, trenches, and bits of pottery and statues. Various tribes lived here as long ago as ten thousand years. The earliest were wandering hunters. After them came a tribe that lived on the shellfish in the area. Gradually groups of Indians who farmed the land settled down and built their homes and temples.

Mound City Group National Monument, in Ohio, and *Effigy*

6

Mounds National Monument, in Iowa, belong to the second area where prehistoric Americans left traces. The monuments preserve widespread burial mounds, each one of which was slowly built up by Indians who had neither shovels nor wheeled vehicles. Workers must have scraped up the earth with bits of shell or bone or sticks, then carried it in rude baskets or animal skins and dumped it load by load on a slowly growing mound. About one million such basketfuls would have been needed to build some of the piles of earth.

Mound City Group was probably heaped up about two thousand years ago. Bracelets, headdresses, ceremonial pipes, and other ornaments have been found buried in the mounds. These objects, along with bits of pottery, are all beautiful; their makers were true artists. Each mound was probably the place where the last rites for an important tribesman were held.

Effigy Mounds are unusual because they are built in the shape of animals and birds. The most common shapes are those of hawks, eagles, bears, and foxes. A few mounds resemble dogs, deer, rabbits, turtles, lizards, and panthers.

The greatest number of prehistoric Indian remains, however, are in the Southwest. Many are in the area around "Four Corners" where the lonely desertlands of Arizona, New Mexico, Colorado, and Utah meet — the only spot in the United States where the boundaries of four states come together. Here, some time between the years A.D. 1 and 1300, an unusual Indian civilization grew for a time, then mysteriously disappeared.

The prehistoric people here were farming Indians at a high point of Stone Age civilization. About the time of Christ's birth, small tribes began to form villages in what is now the Four Corners area. Using primitive tools to work the ground, they grew corn, beans, and squash. At first they lived in shallow caves. Then they dug holes in the ground, put up posts to hold a makeshift roof, and lived in these so-called "pit houses." Still later, they raised the pit

7

houses to the surface of the ground and built rows of rooms where entire families were born, lived, and died.

Some time during the eighth or ninth century these primitive tribes learned to use blocks of stone for building. First they made small dwellings, then large masonry pueblos or "apartment houses," towers, and huge circular rooms called "kivas," which were used for religious ceremonies. These people had no metal tools, nor did they know about wheels. They had no animals they could use as beasts of burden. They cut and carried their heavy building stones by hand. They brought timber for lodgepoles and roofs from mountain forests miles away. They made beautiful pottery, wove complicated designs in cotton cloth, and carved jewelry from brightly colored minerals.

For many generations the Indians lived peacefully. About the year 1200, however, some of them left their villages, which were usually in wide valleys and on the flat tops of mesas. Instead, they moved into narrow canyons protected by steep cliffs. Their pueblos were built in great natural caves in the sides of the cliffs. Some of these canyon "cities" housed as many as four hundred people, a great number for those early days. No one knows for sure why the people moved. Experts think that warlike tribes began to come into the region and to threaten the peaceful farmers. The cliff dwellings gave them better protection.

In the year 1276 a long drought began. Too little rain fell during the twenty-four years that followed. Hot winds blew away the best soil. Crops would not grow. The springs which had provided clear, cool water dried up. Gradually the peaceful tribes left their pueblos and cliff dwellings and wandered south. Possibly they believed that their gods had put a curse on the land. In any case, soon after the year 1300 almost all of them had left.

Fourteen national monuments preserve various ruins of the abandoned villages. Of these, four are in New Mexico. *Aztec*

Pueblo Bonito ruin, Chaco Canyon National Monument, New Mexico. The circles are the remains of kivas. (National Park Service photo)

9

Aztec Ruins National Monument, New Mexico (National Park Service photo)

Ruins National Monument marks one of the largest prehistoric villages. One of its buildings was three stories high and had over five hundred rooms. *Bandelier National Monument,* named for a distinguished Swiss scientist who spent many years studying the site, contains pueblo ruins and a series of cliff dwellings carved in the wall of a hidden canyon. *Chaco Canyon National Monument* seems to have been one of the largest prehistoric towns in America. There are over a dozen large ruins and hundreds of smaller ones. This region was probably a major center of the pre-historic civilization. One of the ruins, Pueblo Bonito, was built five stories high in the shape of a letter D. It had eight hundred rooms in which twelve hundred people lived; it was probably the world's largest prehistoric apartment house. *Gila Cliff Dwellings National Monument* is the well-preserved ruin of rooms built in natural cavities in the face of an overhanging cliff.

Arizona has eight monuments preserving ancient dwellings. One

**Cliff dwelling, Gila Cliff Dwellings National Monument, New Mexico
(National Park Service photo)**

of the most impressive is *Montezuma Castle National Monument.* Most of it is still preserved. Many of its rooms still look just as they must have when they were abandoned about six hundred years ago. The main dwellings were built in the cavity of a great limestone cliff. This apartment house was five stories high and had twenty rooms. Not far away is *Tuzigoot National Monument,* preserving what is left of a village of 110 rooms built on top of a hill overlooking a river valley.

Tonto National Monument is made up of buildings that were placed in a huge natural cave just under the top of a cliff, high up in the wall of a canyon. From this natural fort the Indians could defend themselves against attacking enemies.

In southern Arizona, *Casa Grande National Monument* (the words are Spanish for "great house") is the ruin of a combination apartment house and watchtower six hundred years old. It is four stories high, and made of packed earth instead of rock or stone — the only remaining example of such a building. The Indians who originally lived in the southern part of Arizona are known as the Hohokam, an Indian word meaning "the Ancient Ones." Their way of living was different from that of the Pueblos, who came later. For instance, the Hohokam colored their pottery buff, while the Pueblos colored theirs red, white, and black. The Hohokam's buildings were only one story, with single rooms; the Pueblos' were several stories high. We know that the Casa Grande was a Pueblo building which must have been put up around 1300, when the drought had forced many of the Pueblo tribes to go south in search of useful land.

Walnut Canyon National Monument preserves the ruins of more than three hundred cliff dwellings, most of them dating from the years 1000 to 1200. Using overhanging rock ledges as ceilings, the Indians built their one-room stone houses in natural hollows in the canyon walls.

Cliff dwelling, Montezuma Castle National Monument, Arizona
(National Park Service photo by Natt Dodge)

13

Wupatki National Monument includes the ruins of about eight hundred dwellings, ranging from simple pit houses to three-story hilltop pueblos. Wupatki also has the ruins of a huge amphitheater that was used for religious ceremonies. Besides this, there are two structures that experts think were used as courts for playing a certain kind of ball game. The main pueblos at Wupatki were built about A.D. 1100. A volcanic eruption some time before had spread cinders and ashes over the land, making it so fertile that within a few years many tribes settled in the area in a kind of "land rush."

Navajo National Monument, placed far off by itself in northeastern Arizona, preserves three cliff villages exciting to see. One is Betatakin, a Navajo name meaning "Hillside House." It includes the ruins of 150 rooms, and is seven hundred years old. Betatakin was built on the floor of a giant natural cave in the side of an overhanging cliff. The ceiling of the cave slants far out over the village. The other two communities, Keet Seel and Inscription House, are also built in cliffside caves. They can be reached only by rough

Wupatki ruin, south group, Wupatki National Monument, Arizona
(National Park Service photo by R. J. Fleming)

Keet Seel, prehistoric cliff dwelling, Navajo National Monument, Arizona
(National Park Service photo by George Grant)

horse trails. Besides these villages, there is *Canyon de Chelly National Monument* in the impressive, thousand-foot-deep red rock gorges of today's Navajo Indian Reservation. Several hundred ruined cliff dwellings are scattered in the canyons that cut through the area.

To the north, astride the Utah-Colorado border, is *Hovenweep National Monument*. (Hovenweep is a Ute Indian word meaning "deserted valley.") This monument has the ruins of six groups of pueblos built in and around small, rocky canyons. Most famous of these ruins are the many towers, built in squares, ovals, and circles, which were plainly used as forts to protect the tribes against their enemies. From loopholes in the walls a brave could control the approaches to the trails and the important springs of water.

15

Dinosaur National Monument, also on the Colorado-Utah border, preserves what is left of prehistoric animals rather than prehistoric people. It is on a wild, rugged plateau cut by deep canyons through which race the Green, the Yampa, and other rivers. The area is famous for the fossil remains of great reptiles that roamed this part of the continent millions of years ago. In the Dinosaur Quarry, layers of rock have been cut away to show in relief many huge dinosaur bones. Nearly twenty-six complete skeletons have been uncovered and placed in public museums. The longest skeleton, of a *Diplodocus*, reached 84 feet. Prehistoric Indians lived here, too. Remains of their camps have been found, and some of the canyon walls are covered with their carvings.

Yucca House National Monument, in Colorado, is the only Southwestern prehistoric monument not yet open to the public. Its ruins, a huge Indian pueblo, have not yet been excavated and studied by scientists.

Dinosaur remains as they were uncovered at Dinosaur National Monument, Utah-Colorado (National Park Service photo by A. S. Coggeshall)

This statue of Juan Rodriguez Cabrillo, Portuguese-born discoverer of California, is Portugal's gift to California (National Park Service photo)

Historic Places and People

From time to time in American history various persons have stood out above all others; their courage, loyalty, or devotion to duty have made them the country's heroes. Or, at times, various places have played important parts in history and have become landmarks in America's growth. National monuments have been created to honor many such persons and places. Today there are nineteen such historic monuments.

Cabrillo National Monument, at the tip of a peninsula in San Diego, California, contains a beautiful tablet with a sculptured figure of a ship under full sail. The words on the tablet tell the story of the place.

Here, at Point Loma Head, on the afternoon of September 28, 1542, Juan Rodriguez Cabrillo, distinguished Portuguese navigator in the service of Spain, commanding the flagship San Salvador . . . discovered what is now the State of California . . .

17

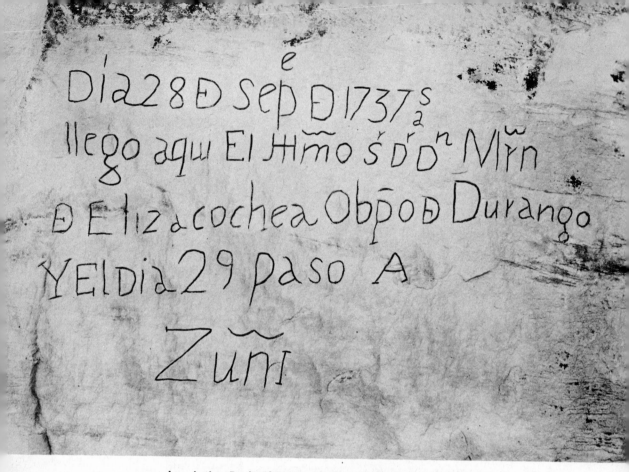

Inscription Rock, El Morro National Monument, New Mexico
(National Park Service photo by George Grant)

Sailing up the Mexican coast in stormy and uncharted waters, Cabrillo made a landfall on the Pacific coast of what is now the United States. He died three months later, and is thought to have been buried on tiny San Miguel, one of the Channel Islands off the coast of Southern California. After his burial his two ships continued farther north to Oregon.

The early Spanish explorers and colonists are recalled in three other national monuments. After military expeditions from Mexico explored what is now the southwest part of the United States,

Spanish missionaries made the dangerous trip to try to convert to European ways the Indians who lived there. *Gran Quivira National Monument,* in New Mexico, preserves the stone ruins of a frontier mission built in 1659. It was abandoned about fifteen years later as a result of drought and the raids of Apache Indians. To the west, in Arizona, later Spanish missionaries built a beautiful mission near a tiny Indian village named Tumacacori. Today *Tumacacori National Monument* is the crumbling but massive church, which was deserted about twenty-five years after Mexico won its freedom from Spain in 1821.

Perhaps most fascinating, however, is *El Morro National Monument,* sometimes called Inscription Rock. El Morro, a huge cliff rising from the desert floor in New Mexico, lay near the old trails to the Indian pueblos and the West. Rain and snow drained from the clifftop into a rocky pool that the desert traveler could always count on for fresh water. Because of this advantage, El Morro became a regular camping spot for missionaries, soldiers, and, later, American pioneers and traders. Hundreds who passed by carved their names into the soft sandstone of the cliff. As a result, El Morro is almost like a "hotel register" of the men and women who pioneered the American West. The first white man to put his name on it was the Spaniard Don Juan de Onate, in 1605. Even before his coming, ancient Indians who lived near it had made hundreds of carvings on the rock. It may seem strange that National Park Service rules forbid present-day visitors to add their names to the list, but this is necessary, of course, in order to protect the historic ones.

As the Spanish grew less powerful in the West, American explorers and pioneers took over. One of the most famous and important of the explorers was Meriwether Lewis, who commanded the Lewis and Clark expedition which set out to cross the unknown wilderness from St. Louis to Oregon in 1804. The expedition trav-

19

eled through unmapped country inhabited by hostile Indian tribes. As they journeyed, Meriwether Lewis and William Clark collected valuable information about the climate and geography, the natural resources, the animals and Indians of nearly half the area that is now the United States. They also discovered and mapped the courses of many important rivers, among them the Missouri, Yellowstone, Snake, and Columbia. Lewis was rewarded by being made governor of the huge Louisiana Territory by President Thomas Jefferson. But he died mysteriously in 1809 at the age of thirty-five, near a small village in central Tennessee. Today at *Meriwether Lewis National Monument* a broken pillar, a symbol of his untimely death, marks Lewis's grave.

Forty years after the Lewis and Clark expedition, pioneers by the thousands were moving west into the region these two men explored. Traders, trappers, and family groups, seeking homes or gold or adventure, rode covered wagons over the famous Oregon Trail; it is a great natural highway that was used for travel even by prehistoric Indians. Scotts Bluff, in western Nebraska, is a huge cliff that made a good landmark and camp site on the trail. Today *Scotts Bluff National Monument* preserves this historic spot. Nearby, wagon ruts show — the actual ones worn into the ground of the Oregon Trail by the thousands of pioneers who traveled over it.

One of the first white women to journey west by way of the Oregon Trail was Narcissa Whitman, wife of a missionary, Marcus Whitman. In 1836 the Whitmans, along with other missionaries, traveled to what is now Washington state to minister to the Indians. For eleven years Marcus and Narcissa Whitman worked in friendship with the natives. They taught them to read and write, and to farm and build. In 1847, however, some of the Indians massacred the Whitmans and twelve other white people and destroyed their mission. Today, near Walla Walla, Washington, *Whitman National*

Log cabin on the site of the first homestead claimed on January 1, 1863,
Homestead National Monument, Nebraska
(National Park Service photo by Jack Boucher)

Monument preserves the ruins of the mission buildings along with the "great grave" where the massacre victims were buried.

By the 1860's, people who were willing to pioneer were rewarded by a gift of free land from the government. The famous Homestead Act became effective on January 1, 1863. It provided that any United States citizen who was twenty-one years or older or who was a head of a family could claim 160 acres of the land that belonged to the government. If he lived on the land for five years and farmed it, he would then own it free and clear. Over a million people settled on land claims in the next sixty years. *Homestead National Monument,* in Nebraska, is at the site of the first claim made under the act. A Civil War Union soldier, Daniel Freeman, filed his claim shortly after midnight on January 1, 1863. When the war ended, Freeman moved to his new land, built a log cabin and later a better home, and lived there with his family until he died in 1908. A typical cabin, furniture, tools used by the pioneers, and the graves of Freeman and his wife are included in the monument.

Pipe Spring National Monument, in northern Arizona, is a well-preserved fort built at a desert spring by early Mormon pioneers to protect themselves against Indian raids. It had a firing platform and loopholes for rifles. The latter can still be seen, along with some of the original tools and furniture. The spring received its name when a group of explorers, including a crack shot named William Hamblin, camped there in 1856. On a bet, Hamblin placed a tobacco pipe on a rock near the spring some distance away. The open part of the pipe bowl faced him. Hamblin said he could shoot out the bottom of the bowl without touching the rim with a bullet. When he made the great shot, the group named the place Pipe Spring.

Pipes also gave their name to *Pipestone National Monument,* in Minnesota. Here the Indians quarried the hardened red clay from which they carved their ceremonial peace pipes. They smoked the pipes at solemn occasions only: when war was ended, treaties made, or chiefs selected. Early Indians considered the quarries sacred places; even enemy tribes camped there in peace. Modern Indians still use the stone. Legends say that two Indian maidens living under the ground guard the quarries. Near the monument is Leaping Rock, formerly used by the Indians in a test for their young men. Young Indians who could jump from Leaping Rock to a polished ridge eleven feet away, and back again, became braves. Those who missed, or slipped, fell twenty feet to the ground.

"We have met the enemy and they are ours." This famous message by Commodore Oliver Hazard Perry is familiar to every American. It announces the defeat of a British fleet on Lake Erie

Perry's Victory and International Peace Memorial National Monument, Ohio
(National Park Service photo by Howard Chapman)

in an important battle of the War of 1812. Not only did the victory help America win the war; it also strengthened the claims of the young United States to the northwestern lands and was one of the events that led to the establishment of the unarmed, peaceful United States-Canadian border. A tall, brilliantly lighted memorial column on a small island in Lake Erie, near the Ohio shore, marks the site of *Perry's Victory and International Peace Memorial National Monument.*

Another wartime memorial is *Harpers Ferry National Monument,* in West Virginia. In 1859 a man named John Brown led a

Andrew Johnson's tailor shop, Andrew Johnson National Monument,
Tennessee (National Park Service photo)

raid on a government armory and gun-making factory at Harpers
Ferry, hoping to rescue and free some slaves. But soldiers killed
or captured most of the raiders, and John Brown was tried and
hanged for treason. The incident was an important one in the
events that led to the Civil War. We are still reminded of it by the
song "John Brown's Body."

Several historic national monuments honor famous Americans.
The *George Washington Birthplace National Monument* preserves
the site of the Virginia plantation home where the first President
of the United States was born.

In Greeneville, Tennessee, the *Andrew Johnson National Monument* includes the original tailor shop, home, and grave of Andrew Johnson, seventeenth President of the United States. John-

24

son's father died when he was four years old. As he grew older, Johnson helped support his family by working as a tailor while he educated himself. Although his childhood was humble, his honesty and belief in democracy won him various political offices until finally he became President after Lincoln was shot.

The *Booker T. Washington National Monument,* near Roanoke, Virginia, is the site of the birthplace and childhood home of a famous Negro. Born a slave, Booker T. Washington worked his way through college as a janitor. After teaching for a few years, he founded Tuskegee College to help train other Negroes. One of his most famous fellow-teachers was George Washington Carver, who had also been born a slave. Carver's parents died when he was young, and he had no money, but he also worked his way through school until he was graduated as an expert in agricultural chemistry. Carver was a genius at chemical research; he discovered how to turn peanuts into more than three hundred useful products ranging from milk to paper. He also developed hundreds of new products made from sweet potatoes, cotton, wood shavings, old sacks, coffee grounds, and even orange peels. By discovering ways of using other crops than cotton, he opened new horizons for Southern farmers, and helped to start many important industries. The *George Washington Carver National Monument,* in Missouri, marks the plantation where he was born in a log cabin.

In the town of West Orange, New Jersey, the *Edison Laboratory National Monument* honors a great American inventor, Thomas A. Edison. Here are the original buildings where Edison and his staff worked during the last forty-four years of his life, and where he invented such marvels as electric motors, the electric locomotive, the camera that led to motion picture cameras, the phonograph, and hundreds of other things. The monument buildings today contain Edison's own desk, his notebooks and letters, many early phonograph records, many early kinds of electric light bulbs,

25

and thousands of other items ranging from a tiny light-bulb filament to a huge dynamo. Do you know what Edison's first phonograph said? "Mary had a little lamb . . ."

The Statue of Liberty in New York Harbor is another national monument. When the French sculptor Frédéric Bartholdi sailed up the harbor on his first trip to America he decided that here, at the gateway to the New World, was the very spot to put the spirit of liberty. He started the plan that resulted in his statue's being presented as a gift from France to America to mark the long friendship between the two nations. The torch of freedom, held high in Liberty's upraised hand, has been a welcome sight to millions of people coming to settle in America in search of freedom and justice.

The Statue of Liberty, one of the largest in the world, is 151 feet tall, and stands on a base that is itself 154 feet high. Liberty's face is 10 feet wide. The arm holding the torch is 42 feet long and 12 feet wide at its thickest point. Visitors who take the short ferry ride from Manhattan's Battery to Liberty Island can climb a spiral stairway to the very head of the statue.

At the other end of the country in America's forty-ninth state, Alaska, *Sitka National Monument* reminds Americans of another part of their nation's history. At this spot a village of Sitka Indians fought valiantly until they were defeated by a group of early Russian fur trappers and traders. The Russians made the region the center of their settlements in Alaska. After the United States bought the area from Russia in 1867, Sitka remained the capital until 1906. The monument now marks the site of the Indians' fort and displays eighteen of the world's finest totem poles. A totem pole is a tall wooden shaft on which some Indian tribes of northwestern North America carved and painted figures which told the story of family and tribal events, or which pictured legends about

Statue of Liberty at night, Statue of Liberty National Monument, New York
(National Park Service photo by Ralph Anderson)

27

Totem poles, Sitka National Monument, Alaska (National Park Service photo)

the creation of the earth and its birds and animals. The "Fog Women" totem pole at Sitka, 59 feet high, is one of the world's tallest.

Forts and Battlefields

Scattered across the United States are sites recalling brave days in our country's history. Crumbling but still grim-looking forts, ancient cannon, the remains of cavalry stables and barracks, cemeteries that lie peacefully in former Indian battlegrounds all are vivid reminders of the past.

The fourteen forts and battlefields that have been named as national monuments represent periods in America's growth ranging from the early days of settlement on the Florida coast to the years when the pioneers struggled westward to the Pacific Ocean. Each has its own fascinating story to tell.

Two ancient forts in Florida and another in Georgia mark the days when the Spanish, the French, and the English were fighting for control of the New World. The oldest fort is at *Fort Matanzas National Monument,* in Florida. The fort itself was built by the Spanish forces near St. Augustine in 1742, to guard the southern approaches of the town against Oglethorpe's English colony in Georgia. But its story began two centuries earlier.

After Columbus's discoveries in the New World, Spanish adventurers, soldiers, and priests flocked to the Western Hemisphere. The Caribbean region bustled with merchants, sailors, and pirates. Spanish galleons, filled with gold, silver, pearls, and other treasures, sailed home along the Gulf Stream. In going northward they kept close to the coast of Florida in order to pick up the fast ocean current and to gain protection against pirates. Hence it was important for the Spanish to control the settlements in Florida.

Very early they established a colony at St. Augustine. The leaders of a nearby French colony attacked the Spanish in 1565, but the French fleet was destroyed in a storm and the Spanish massacred the survivors. To prevent other attacks the Spanish built a blockhouse and watchtower at Matanzas. Each time soldiers

Fort Matanzas National Monument, Florida (National Park Service photo by J. Carver Harris)

sighted a strange ship, a runner was sent with the news to St. Augustine, fourteen miles to the north.

In 1683 pirates landed and captured the sentries at Matanzas. The pirates started to march on St. Augustine, but one Spanish soldier escaped and warned the townspeople. Soldiers streamed out of another fort guarding St. Augustine, and ambushed the unsuspecting pirates. This fort is now *Castillo de San Marcos National Monument,* also in Florida. It took twenty-five years to build, from 1672 to 1696. Its walls were 30 feet high and 12 feet thick.

Castillo de San Marcos National Monument, Florida
(National Park Service photo)

31

Fort Frederica National Monument, Georgia (National Park Service photo by Gil Tharp)

About the time the Spanish built their fort at Matanzas British settlers in Georgia, under General James Oglethorpe, built a fort of their own, just north of St. Augustine. We know it today as *Fort Frederica National Monument.* When Spain and England went to war in 1739, soldiers from Fort Frederica besieged the Castillo de San Marcos. But the Spanish managed to get food and ammunition through the blockade, and the English eventually had to retreat. Two years later the Spanish attacked Fort Frederica, but they too had to give up. Eventually, in 1821, Spain yielded the troublesome Florida territory to the United States.

The Castillo was used for a while as a prison. Fort Matanzas and Fort Frederica decayed into ruins. Cannon were dismounted from the crumbling walls, and the towers fell. Today visitors to these three national monuments can relive a stirring period of our country's history as they wander through the ancient barracks and gun rooms.

The War of 1812, between England and the young United States, accounted for two more forts that are now national monuments. In 1811 Castle Clinton was built at the foot of Manhattan Island, to defend New York City against possible attack. It had twenty-eight cannon, and eight-foot-thick walls built in the shape of a circle. It was never attacked. Perhaps, simply by being there it kept the British from trying to capture the city.

When the war was over, the fort was renamed Castle Garden and was turned into an auditorium for concerts, exhibitions, operas, and other entertainments. Later, during the years when hundreds of thousands of people were immigrating into America, Castle Garden became a landing depot for the newcomers. Later still, the old fort became New York's famous Aquarium. After World War II the building was scheduled to be destroyed, to make way for a tunnel linking Manhattan and Brooklyn. But New Yorkers who appreciated the building's history protested and the old fort was preserved as *Castle Clinton National Monument.*

Perhaps best known of all the early forts is Fort McHenry, which inspired the writing of our national anthem. The fort, at the tip of Baltimore, Maryland, was built after the Revolutionary War. During the War of 1812 the British captured Washington and marched on Baltimore. A British fleet steamed into Chesapeake Bay and began to shell the fort. During a bombardment of twenty-five hours the British ships sent 1,800 shells, bombs, and rockets into the stronghold. But the defenders held out, drove back a landing attempt, and forced the British to withdraw from the city.

Fort McHenry National Monument, Maryland (National Park Service photo)

All during the anxious night of September 13, 1814, an American, Francis Scott Key, waited on a boat in the rear of the British fleet. He was a lawyer who had been trying to reach an agreement with the British for the release of a war prisoner, and was held on the boat overnight. During the day he had seen the American flag flying over the fort as it was bombarded. During the night, however, the British stopped firing so that they could try a landing. Key was worried, thinking the silence might mean Fort McHenry had surrendered. But at dawn on September 14 he saw the flag still flying. On the back of an old letter he set down the first words of his poem, "The Star-Spangled Banner": *"Oh, say can you see by the dawn's early light, what so proudly we hailed at the twilight's last gleaming?"* Soon the poem was set to the music of an old English tune. Although it became popular, it did not officially become our national anthem until 1931.

In time, Fort McHenry became a prison and then a veterans' hospital. Today it is a national monument. Its bombardment is "reenacted" each year to commemorate the fort's historic battle. Recent researchers, guided by old maps, have uncovered oak timbers that they think may have formed the base of the original flagpole from which the star-spangled banner flew.

Three more forts won fame during the Civil War. Best known is *Fort Sumter National Monument.* This five-sided fort, built on a shoal in the Charleston, South Carolina, harbor, was occupied by federal troops when South Carolina seceded from the Union and helped to form the Confederacy. In April, 1861, a Union ship carrying food and weapons for the men in the fort neared Charleston, and Confederate guns fired at Fort Sumter. For nearly two days the Union men took a bombardment of three thousand shells. Then, with the fort badly damaged and their ammunition gone, the Union forces surrendered. A day later the Civil War began. In 1863 a Union attempt to capture Fort Sumter failed. The blockade and siege continued for two years before Fort Sumter yielded, shortly before the war was to end.

In the nineteenth century a massive fort was built on an island on the coast of Savannah, Georgia, and was named in honor of Polish Count Casimir Pulaski, who fought for America during the Revolutionary War. From 1829 to 1847 nearly a million dollars was spent to put in place 25,000,000 bricks which were supposed to make Fort Pulaski unbeatable. When Georgia joined the Confederacy in 1861, its troops took over Fort Pulaski. They believed shells could not damage it seriously. But the Union forces had a

Guns on west flank, Fort Sumter National Monument, South Carolina
(National Park Service photo by Arthur Fawcett)

Fort Pulaski National Monument, Georgia (National Park Service
photo by Jack Boucher)

new weapon: cannon with rifled barrels that could fire shells
harder and farther than ever before. In less than two days of bombardment the Union cannon breached the fort and forced it to
surrender. As a result, Savannah, a major Confederate port, was
cut off for the rest of the Civil War. *Fort Pulaski National Monument* preserves the remnants of this building which became a landmark in military history; its defeat proved that old-fashioned brick
and masonry forts could not stand up against modern guns.

Fort Jefferson National Monument contains the ruins of a great
fort built on a sandy island in the Gulf of Mexico, off the tip of the

Corner bastion, the moat, and Gulf of Mexico, Fort Jefferson
National Monument, Florida (National Park Service photo)

Florida Keys. Work on it started in 1846 and, though it went on for thirty years, was never really finished because the foundations began to settle in the loose sand.

Union troops occupied Fort Jefferson during the Civil War, but there was no military action. After the war, the fort was used as a prison. Its most famous prisoner was Dr. Samuel A. Mudd, a man who unknowingly committed the act of a traitor in the following manner. When John Wilkes Booth, the man who shot Lincoln, was trying to escape from the scene he broke his leg. Dr. Mudd did not know what Booth had done and set his leg for him, thinking this his duty as a doctor. Mudd was arrested for his act, and was sentenced to life imprisonment. When a yellow fever epidemic struck Fort Jefferson, Dr. Mudd worked night and day at the risk of his own life to help save others. Shortly afterward he was pardoned and freed.

From time to time over the years the United States Navy tried to establish a base at Fort Jefferson, but fires and storms damaged the buildings. Eventually the island was left to the weather and the birds. Today the Fort Jefferson National Monument includes the seven Dry Tortugas Islands and the surrounding waters in the Gulf of Mexico. Tropical birds — sooty terns, noddy terns, huge frigate birds, and boobies — nest there by the thousands. Brilliantly colored tropical fish swim lazily among the coral reefs that dot the blue waters.

As the pioneers, the gold-seekers, and the traders headed for America's western prairies and mountains, forts were necessary to help protect them from the Indians whose lands they were overrunning. In the nineteenth century the largest United States military fort to guard the southwest frontier was Fort Union, on the famous Santa Fe Trail, in New Mexico. Today *Fort Union National Monument* is mostly ruins; but enough of the old walls and foundations remain to give us some picture of the key military post where such men as General Grant, General Sherman, and Colonel Kit Carson served.

Fort Union protected settlers and travelers from war parties of Utes, Comanches, and Apaches. It was also a supply center for outlying posts. Even today the wheel-tracks of the thousands of covered wagons that rolled across the land can still be seen as ruts in the ground.

Eventually, when there were no longer enough buffalo left on the plains to support the Indians, the tribes began to weaken and die. By necessity they gave up the warpath for the reservation. For a while Fort Union was a station on a stagecoach route. It was abandoned in 1891.

To the north, in Wyoming, the Oregon Trail was traveled by other thousands who sought gold and land in the West. They too needed protection from Indians. An early fort that had been built to protect fur traders was bought by the government and made into an army post called Fort Laramie. In 1851 more than 10,000 In-

39

dians gathered at the fort to sign a treaty with the white men. After years of bad feeling there was another peace treaty in 1868. But when the discovery of gold in the Black Hills once more brought miners into Indian hunting grounds, the white men broke the treaty. The Indians fought, but were finally subdued. When Fort Laramie was abandoned, its buildings were sold to homesteaders. Eventually the historic importance of the fort was recognized, however, and it was named *Fort Laramie National Monument*.

Fort Vancouver National Monument marks the site of a fort built by the British in 1829 on the Columbia River in southern Washington. It protected trappers and traders of the great Hudson's Bay Company, which controlled fur trade in the Northwest. Although built as a fort, Vancouver never fired a gun in defense. The local Indians were friendly, and the fort served mostly as a business and social center for the region. When Oregon and Washington became American territory, the fort was turned over to the United States Army.

Three Indian battlefields are also national monuments. The oldest is *Ackia Battleground National Monument*. On the site of a Chickasaw Indian village in Mississippi, it marks the Battle of Ackia, May 26, 1736, in which the Chickasaws and their British allies defeated the Choctaw Indians, who were supported by the French.

Big Hole Battlefield National Monument, in Montana, was the scene of a famous Indian battle in 1877. During that year Chief Joseph, a valiant Nez Percé Indian, led about seven hundred braves, squaws, and children in an attempt to escape to Canada rather than be forced onto a reservation. At the Big Hole River the party was attacked by United States troops. Chief Joseph and some of his people escaped and fled south, then east and north toward Canada, going through Yellowstone National Park on the way. But another army group trapped them in Montana and forced them to sur-

40

Officers' quarters and sutler's store, Fort Laramie National Monument, Wyoming (National Park Service photo)

render. Said Chief Joseph, weary and sick at heart: "From where the sun now stands, I will fight no more, forever."

Most famous of all Indian battles was the Battle of the Little Big Horn River, also known as "Custer's Last Stand." Tribesmen were resentful of white prospectors and soldiers who swarmed over lands that had been promised to the Indians by treaty; they went on the warpath in 1876. Three columns of United States troops were sent to battle them. Lieutenant Colonel George A. Custer, a famous Indian fighter, decided to attack at once. But there were more Indian braves than he had expected. Outnumbered and cut off from reinforcements, Custer and all his men were killed in a gallant stand. Today *Custer Battlefield National Monument* includes the battlefield and a small national cemetery.

Shifting patterns in the sand, Great Sand Dunes National Monument, Colorado (National Park Service photo by Natt Dodge)

Deserts

Not all the deserts of the world are far away, like the Sahara, in Africa, or the Gobi, in Asia. America has its deserts, too — hot, dry wastes where the sun beats down on strange landscapes thinly scattered with plants.

Three desert regions are so unusual that they have been named national monuments. One, *Great Sand Dunes National Monument* in southern Colorado, has some of the highest desert sand dunes

42

in the country. Many ages ago this region was the coastline of an inland sea. Then great earth movements gradually lifted a range of mountains, now called the Sangre de Cristo. Sand and gravel were deposited in the valley at the base of the mountains, and volcanoes threw out lava and ashes. Some of the lava blocked off one end of the valley. As the centuries passed, the wind, which almost always sweeps across the valley from the southwest, carried the light sands with it. But the 14,000-foot barrier of the Sangre de Cristo range, like a giant hand, turns the wind upward, forcing it to drop its burden of sand at the foot of the mountains. Today the grains of sand have piled up into dunes that tower as much as six hundred feet above the floor of the valley.

The pressure of the wind constantly changes the shape and position of the dunes. Over the years they actually move. It happens like this. The wind blows millions of sand grains up one side of a dune. At the crest, the grains fall over to the protected slope, building that side up. Eventually this causes the crest of the dune to move forward. At times the dunes may bury a group of pine trees. When the sand has passed, the trees appear again as skeletons, stripped bare of their leaves and branches.

Another remarkable desert area is *White Sands National Monument,* in New Mexico. Its gleaming dunes look like mounds of snow. Actually they are made of crystals of gypsum, a white mineral. During the day the contrasting sunlight and shadow on the pure white sands is striking. At night, beneath the moon, the dunes look weird and ghostly.

The valley where White Sands lies is surrounded by beds of gypsum. Rain and snow dissolve the mineral, which collects in a lake. When the summer heat causes the gypsum-laden lake to evaporate, crystals of gypsum are left. The wind whirls them away to form the dunes, which constantly grow and move. Some plants manage to survive the march of the earth by growing very long

**Close-up of drifting sand, White Sands National Monument, New Mexico
(National Park Service photo)**

stems that enable them to keep their "heads" above the sand. In some places they have been found with stems 40 feet long.

The whiteness of the gypsum desert has had a strange effect on the few lizards and mice that live in the area. Over the centuries only the lighter-colored animals have survived; the darker ones were easily spotted against the light background and were killed by enemies. Thus, gradually, the unusual white lizards and mice that live in White Sands have become the typical ones for that place. Although the mice that live in the dunes are white, those that live in nearby reddish hills are red; and another species that lives in neighboring black lava beds has black coats.

The largest and most spectacular of the desert national monu-

44

ments is Death Valley. The Indians who knew this long, narrow valley in eastern California called it "Tomesha," meaning "ground afire." And no wonder. The second highest temperature ever recorded in the world was reached in Death Valley: a searing 134°F. (The record is 136.4°F., set in Libya, Africa.) Although Death Valley is an oven in the summer, its climate is pleasant from October to May. Higher up in the mountains that enclose the valley, nights are often actually cold. Death Valley is a place of extremes. One spot, near a region called Badwater, is 282 feet below sea level; it is the lowest land in the Western Hemisphere. But only a few miles away towers Telescope Peak, more than 11,000 feet high.

Death Valley's history goes back to earliest geologic times. Over millions of years the region was a place of mountains, volcanoes, seas, and lakes. Ten million years ago mastodons and other now-extinct creatures came to drink at the shores of the lakes, and

Gullied gravel and lava lake beds, Death Valley National Monument, California-Nevada (National Park Service photo by Rowe and Schackleton)

left fossil footprints in the mud. When one ancient lake evaporated, blocks of dried salt remained. Later the blocks eroded into a crazy quilt of needlelike ridges, now a tourist attraction called the Devils Golf Course.

The first white people to enter Death Valley were pioneers seeking a route to the California gold fields in 1849. Lost, hungry, and weary, they struggled into the valley in wintertime. Some found a way out through a hidden canyon. Others suffered unimaginable hardship as they crossed the salt flats. Many died on the way. One group, it is said, looked back across the terrible sands from the safety of the mountain peaks, and gave the place its name when they said, "Good-by, Death Valley."

As the region became more familiar, prospectors sought gold in the mountains around the valley. Towns with quaint names like Skiddoo and Chloride City were settled, boomed briefly, then turned into ghost towns which are still visited by tourists. No one found gold. But some found borax, a salt useful to certain industries. Miners used high-wheeled wagons drawn by twenty mules to get the borax out of the valley. But soon other borax deposits were found in more convenient places. Death Valley would have become deserted again except for the doings of a colorful character called Death Valley Scotty, an ex-cowboy who built a "castle" in the valley and opened it to tourists.

Although Death Valley seems to be a lifeless place, many animals live there: squirrels, rats, rabbits, foxes, bighorn sheep, wild burros, lizards, birds, and even a kind of fish called "desert sardine." Many of these animals roam the valley at night, and get their water from plants they eat. There are hundreds of species of plants, most of which survive the dry, hot summers by shedding their leaves and sinking roots very deep into the ground. If there has been a fair amount of rain during the winter, Death Valley in the spring is a riot of colorful flowers.

View of saguaro cactus plants, Saguaro National Monument, Arizona
(National Park Service photo by George Grant)

Plants and Animals

Five national monuments have been created chiefly to preserve and encourage the growth of rare kinds of plants and animals, and to enable tourists to see them in their native surroundings.

Three of these regions are the homes of unusual desert plants. Near Tucson, Arizona, is *Saguaro National Monument,* a cactus forest growing at the foot of three rugged mountain ranges. This monument contains one of America's largest stands of giant saguaro (sa-WAH-ro) cactus, a huge plant shaped like a fluted column that may grow to a height of 50 feet. Instead of leaves on its tough green skin the saguaro has spiny needles; they help serve as protection against desert animals who might otherwise eat the plants for their moisture.

A full-grown saguaro weighs about eight tons and can store one ton of water in its pulpy tissues. Its immense root system sucks up water during the short rainy season. During the long, dry hot spell the plant depends on its stored water. Sometimes saguaros store so much liquid that they actually burst.

The saguaro has white flowers at the top of its stems. In the summer these blooms ripen to crimson fruit filled with black seeds. Birds, along with some chipmunks and squirrels, eat the saguaro fruits. Desert Indian tribes used to live on them too, and some still make a drink from the boiled juice of the fruit.

Still deeper in southwestern Arizona is *Organ Pipe Cactus National Monument,* the home of another rare desert plant. The organ pipe is the second largest cactus in America. One plant may have as may as thirty arms that rise straight up from the ground like the pipes of an organ. In the spring it blossoms into lavender and white flowers that open at night and close in the morning. Wild pig, deer, antelope, fox, and coyote roam this area, along with the desert tortoise and the poisonous Gila monster.

Farther to the west, in the desert country of southern California, is *Joshua Tree National Monument,* home of the third unusual type of desert plant. The Joshua tree, a thick, bushy member of the lily family, grows as high as 40 feet. Its many branches jut out at sharp angles from the trunk. Sometimes the plant looks as if it

Joshua trees, Joshua Tree National Monument, California
(National Park Service photo by George Grant)

were praying with upstretched arms. Because of its praying appearance, the Mormons named it Joshua, after the Biblical hero.

Joshua Tree National Monument includes other unusual desert plants with strange names: paloverde, manzanita, ocotillo, indigo bush, smokethorn, and catclaw. Where springs bubble up through the warm sands, clumps of palm trees grow, forming green oases.

From lookout points one can see outside the monument to the Salton Sea, an inland body of water which is 241 feet below sea level. Along the road that loops through the area is the fantastic Wonderland of Rocks. A wall of these rocks completely surrounds Hidden Valley, the hide-out of cattle rustlers in the days of the Old West.

Muir Woods National Monument is a cool, green grove of redwood trees just north of San Francisco. Redwoods grow only along the coast of northern California and are the world's tallest trees. One, 364 feet high, is the tallest living thing on earth. The redwood is not the same plant as the giant sequoia, or big tree, which grows only in the Sierra Nevada range of eastern California. Both trees belong to the same family; but the giant sequoia, while not so tall as a redwood, is much bigger round the trunk and lives longer. Some sequoias are nearly four thousand years old, while redwoods rarely live for more than two thousand years. Redwood Creek runs through the Muir Woods Monument; in the spring one can see trout and salmon fighting their way upstream over its rapids to their spawning grounds.

Rare animals are protected on *Channel Islands National Monument*. The Channel Islands are a group of eight off the coast of Southern California. Two of them, Anacapa Island and Santa Barbara Island, make up the monument. Both are rocky, lonesome spots, often shrouded in fog. The ocean sweeps over the narrowest parts of Anacapa in two places, so separating it into three tiny islets.

Special permission from the National Park Service is needed in order to visit the Channel Islands. Permission is necessary because the monument is a refuge for sea elephants, sea lions, seals, and sea otters. The latter two of these animals had been almost wiped out by hunters, but are now gradually increasing in numbers. The islands are also nesting grounds for hordes of gulls and California brown pelicans. On the eastern tip of Anacapa are an important

50

South shore of Anacapa Island, Channel Islands National Monument, California (National Park Service photo by Roger Toll)

lighthouse and a weather forecasting station. Brave men and their families man these stations all year round, doing their jobs despite loneliness and harsh weather.

51

Woodland path, Muir Woods National Monument, California
(National Park Service photo)

Caves

Three of America's largest underground cave systems are national parks: Carlsbad Caverns in New Mexico, Mammoth Cave in Kentucky, and Wind Cave in South Dakota. Four smaller, but just as beautiful, caves have been made national monuments. All of these caves were formed by the same natural process.

Many millions of years ago inland seas or huge inland lakes covered much of the area of our present-day Western and Midwestern states. Thick deposits of material from animal skeletons were deposited on the ocean and lake beds and hardened into limestone, a kind of rock. Later, tremendous heat and pressure within the earth lifted the earth's crust into mountains. The limestone of the lake and ocean beds became part of the mountain ranges. Rain water found its way into the many cracks and openings in the rock. For countless thousands of years it poured through them, slowly dissolving the limestone and widening the tiny openings into tunnels and, in time, into huge caverns.

The water gradually drained out of the openings it had carved, but it continued to drip from their ceilings. As it evaporated, the lime it carried was deposited on the walls, ceilings, or floors of the caves. Slowly the deposits of limestone grew, sometimes as little as an inch every thousand years. Where a limestone deposit grew downward from the ceiling, like an icicle, it formed what we call a stalactite. Where it grew upward from the floor, it formed what we call a stalagmite. (To make sure you remember the difference, memorize this trick: "Stalactite" is spelled with a "c" for "ceiling"; "stalagmite" is spelled with a "g" for "ground.") Sometimes the two formations joined, to form a floor-to-ceiling pillar. Sometimes limestone seeped from the walls of caves to form delicate stone draperies, ribbonlike strips, or fluted columns.

In time, openings to many of the caves were discovered, often by

Cave formations, Oregon Caves National Monument, Oregon
(National Park Service photo)

accident. A wounded bear helped to uncover *Oregon Caves National Monument*, high in the Siskiyou Mountains of southwestern Oregon. The bear, shot by a hunter named Elijah Davidson, crawled into a narrow opening in the rocks. Davidson hurriedly lighted a torch and followed, to discover a network of passages and

54

weirdly beautiful limestone formations. Early visitors gave descriptive names to some of the fantastic shapes: Garden of the Gods, Neptune's Grotto, Ghost Chamber, and Satan's Cradle.

Another hunter found the opening to *Timpanogos Cave National Monument*, a series of small underground rooms hollowed out of 12,000-foot Mount Timpanogos, which towers southeast of Salt Lake City, Utah. Minerals in the limestone deposits give the Timpanogos formations a rainbow of color, from chocolate-colored "waterfalls" to the reddish "Great Heart of Timpanogos," a heart-shaped stalactite near the center of the cave.

In neighboring Nevada is *Lehman Caves National Monument*, which lies under the flank of 13,000-foot Wheeler Peak in high desert country. A pioneer homesteader named Absalom Lehman discovered the cavern when his horse fell into a hole in the ground. Later explorers found bits of human bones near the entrance; here is possible evidence that prehistoric Indians may have used the caves as a burial chamber. Most famous of Lehman Caves' formations are the "tom-toms," disks of limestone that were deposited on the ceilings. When they are tapped, they sound like an Indian tom-tom.

The smallest of the caverns is *Jewel Cave National Monument*, in South Dakota. Years ago the whistle of wind blowing out of a small hole in a cliff attracted the attention of two prospectors. Hoping to discover minerals, the men widened the opening and discovered the cave. Jewel Cave is unlike the others in that its walls are lined with gemlike crystals of the mineral calcite.

One final word about caves. If you want to know what true darkness is like, wait until you stand in a cavern while the National Park Service ranger turns out the lights. The complete absence of light is like no darkness you have ever known before. Every visitor to a cavern national park or monument stands in awe until the lights come on again.

Cave formations mirrored in water, Lehman Caves National Monument,
Nevada (National Park Service photo by A. Brown)

Craters, Volcanoes, and Lava Flows

Volcanoes, with their mysterious rumblings, rivers of red-hot lava, explosions of rock and ash, and their deep craters, are among the most amazing things in nature. Because the only American volcanoes active at the present time are in far-off Alaska and Hawaii, most Americans do not usually think of their country as a volcanic one. Many thousands of years ago, however, and up until comparatively recent times, the western parts of the continent were the scene of violent eruptions. The results of these outbursts — massive craters, strange flows of hardened lava, and weird rock formations — are preserved today in a variety of remarkable national monuments.

Sunset Crater National Monument, in Arizona, is a reminder of the violent changes that once rocked that region. Great pressures built up under the earth until finally they blasted tons of ash, lava, and cinders through a crack in a mountain and into the sky. By checking the growth rings of trees buried in the ashes, scientists have estimated that the eruptions continued in this area until nine hundred years ago. When they were over, a smoking "cinder cone" 1,000 feet high towered over the landscape. Out of its summit was blown a red and orange crater. Dunes of cinders and ash, and heaps of twisted lava surrounded the cone.

The story of *Capulin Mountain National Monument,* in New Mexico, is much the same. It is a cinder cone about 1,000 feet high, built up by a series of eruptions that ended seven thousand years ago. A bowl-shaped crater sits in the top of the mountain. Sunset Crater's slopes are mostly made up of loose cinders which furnish no rooting ground for plants; but the sides of older Capulin Mountain are covered with trees and bushes. Rare golden eagles soar above its summit. A footpath circles the rim, and another leads down into the bottom of the crater. From the top of Capulin

57

Tree curled by lava flow, Craters of the Moon National Monument, Idaho
(Union Pacific Railroad photo)

Mountain one can see into five states: New Mexico, Colorado, Kansas, Oklahoma, and Texas.

In Central Idaho is the *Craters of the Moon National Monument*, a region of cinder cones, strange lava formations, and mountains of rocks and ashes. A visitor to this bleak and dusty plain can form a good notion of how the surface of the moon may actually appear. Here, in Idaho, over many ancient eons, molten lava poured out of great cracks in the ground. In some places, explosions helped form cinder cones. Lumps of hardened lava made what are called spatter cones, each with a small hole in the top that widens below into a crater like an upside-down funnel.

The eruptions at Craters of the Moon were not violent blasts. As the lava oozed out of the earth like hot molasses, some of the flows broke up into jagged chunks of rock; others cooled to look like thick twisted ropes — or, from the top of a cinder cone, like rivers. Nature played strange tricks with the flows. Sometimes the outside of the lava stream cooled and hardened while the still-molten lava inside drained away, so making lava tubes, or tunnels. When part of the "wall" or "roof" collapsed, a lava bridge or lava cave was formed. Nowadays rain and snow collect in some caves to form ice that lasts all summer. There are also "lava bombs," tear-drop-shaped blobs of lava; and "tree molds," hollow cylinders of lava that were left after a molten flow surrounded a tree trunk, hardened, and completely burned away the wood.

An ancient Indian trail winds through the Craters of the Moon, hinting some truth to legends that Indians formerly lived in the lava caves, or took refuge there.

A similar wild, rocky region is *Lava Beds National Monument,* in California near the Oregon border. Here cinder cones and lava tubes help form a rugged landscape. Of the many large lava caves, one has a frozen waterfall and a river of ice. In some of the caves and on some of the rocks are prehistoric Indian writings, either drawings, called pictographs, or carvings, called petroglyphs.

Lava Beds was the scene of a famous Indian war, the Modoc War of 1872-73. When a handful of Modocs, led by a chief called Captain Jack, rebelled against being sent to a reservation, they took refuge in the caves of the lava country. There they held off

Devils Postpile National Monument, California (National Park Service photo)

the federal soldiers for six months before they were defeated. One natural lava trench is still called Captain Jack's Stronghold.

Devils Postpile National Monument, formed by a lava flow in the high mountains of eastern California, is a giant mass of six-sided pillars of stone. The rock columns rise 60 feet high, and fit together like a giant cluster of posts. They are the result of cracking in the lava flow as it cooled, about 100,000 years ago. Later a glacier covered the columns and, as it advanced, carried many of them away one by one. When the Ice Age ended, the Devils Postpile was the largest group of columns left. Some of the monument's pillars curve or slant; others have fallen, and lie in fragments at the foot of the pile. At the top, where the grinding of the glacier wore the rock smooth, the tops of the six-sided pillars look like a mosaic.

To see one region where underground fires still burn and where volcanoes still are capable of blasting off, one may go to the wild, lonesome part of Alaska where *Katmai National Monument* sprawls amid glacier-covered mountain ranges. This area is the largest in the National Park system. Since the nearest sizable city is two hundred miles away across impassable ground, Katmai can be reached only by plane or boat.

From an airplane one can see the ice-choked bays and fiords along the coast, the mysterious volcanic ash deposits of the Valley of Ten Thousand Smokes, and the magnificent jade-green lake that fills Mount Katmai's hollow basin. The mountain's summit collapsed inward in 1912; although its walls are draped with year-round snow, the lake never freezes because of the volcanic fires that still burn deep inside Katmai.

The eruptions of 1912 sent ashes and a frothy lava called pumice bursting from Novarupta volcano at Katmai monument. Ashes and dust formed a thin haze in the sky over half the world that summer. As a result the weather was colder than usual not

61

Volcanic crater, Katmai National Monument, Alaska
(National Park Service photo)

only in America but in Asia, Europe, and parts of Africa. During the eruptions white-hot ash poured into a nearby valley of forests and streams and flowed like a river for 15 miles, destroying everything in its path. When it stopped, it formed a layer 100 feet thick. Gas and steam from buried streams poured up out of thousands of "fumaroles," small openings in the ground. The steaming holes gave the area its name, Valley of Ten Thousand Smokes.

Gradually these fumaroles have died out, and now plants are beginning to grow at the edge of the volcanic ash. The crater of Novarupta volcano is choked off by a plug of gray rock. All is quiet, for the time being, in the nearly uncharted wilderness of Katmai National Monument.

Scenic Wonders

Thirteen national monuments in our western states have been formed by natural forces, all except one in the following way. Prehistoric seas or lakes covered the areas and laid down layer after layer of silt, sand, and mud. Over the ages these layers hardened into various rock formations. Then came great pressures in the earth, and huge masses of the original rocks were slowly raised and tilted high above their former position. Finally the cliffs and mountains that they formed were worn away. Wind, frost, and rain nibbled at the softer layers of rock. Tiny plants gained footholds in crevices. Temperature changes — extreme heat and cold — cracked some of the rock. Streams and creeks and rivers, with their burdens of sand and gravel, ground away the rock that lined their banks.

As the rocks were worn away, deep canyons developed, and so did immense cliffs, giant amphitheaters, rock towers and archways, and other strangely shaped formations. Many of the layers in the formations have traces of different minerals, which cause them to take on rich colors: red, orange, yellow, or purple. During the day the colors seem to change as the sun moves across the sky. Under the moonlight the jagged cliffs and knife-edged spires gleam alongside the black shadows of the canyons.

One of the largest of the scenic areas is *Badlands National Monument* in South Dakota. Here the rocks of the rugged cliffs and pinnacles are at least 40 million years old. Fossils found in the rock layers show that prehistoric animals roamed the region, among them the saber-toothed tiger, the tiny three-toed horse, and the huge titanothere, which resembles a rhinoceros in some ways and an elephant in others. The Indians who hunted in the western plains called these rocky labyrinths *mako sica,* which means "bad land." The pioneers who settled the region called it "Badlands."

View over Badlands National Monument, South Dakota
(National Park Service photo by Jack Boucher)

Colorado National Monument, in the southwestern part of that state, is another area where cliffs, canyons, and columns were carved as the rock wore away. Most of the rock is red sandstone; *colorado* is a Spanish word for "red." Fossil remains show that such giant dinosaurs as the *Brontosaurus,* the giraffelike *Brachiosaurus,* the *Allosaurus,* the armor-plated *Stegosaurus,* and the huge *Diplodocus* lived in the monument vicinity. Today Rim Rock Drive runs along the edge of the three major canyons and provides views of such weird formations as Window Rock, Devil's Kitchen, Squaw Fingers, Cleopatra's Couch, and Cold Shivers Point.

In southern Utah, tourists driving across the little-known, desert-like region sometimes are certain they see a mirage on the horizon. It may look like a city of red, green, and gray skyscraper buildings rising out of nowhere. Or it may seem to be a group of giant statues looking out over the land. Actually it is *Capitol Reef National Monument*, a huge rock mass worn away so that the sandstone domes that top it look like those of many of our state and national capitol buildings. Here is a wilderness of colored cliffs, and desert canyons called "washes."

Capitol Reef is a great fold in the earth's crust; throughout its

View down Monument Canyon, Colorado National Monument, Colorado
(National Park Service photo by George Grant)

The Great Organ, Capitol Reef National Monument, Utah
(National Park Service photo by George Grant)

150-mile length it can be crossed in only three places by horseback and in only one by car. The motor road, through Capitol Wash, winds through a canyon so narrow that cars can pass each other only at certain spots. The first man to pioneer this road spent eight days in traveling three and one-half miles.

Not far from Capitol Reef is *Cedar Breaks National Monument*, an enormous amphitheater worn in the colored rock. Here are the famous Pink Cliffs; forty-seven different shades of pink have been counted. The region was discovered by Mormon settlers who mistook the many juniper trees for cedars, and gave the name "breaks" to the sharp-edged cliffs and canyons.

Utah's most famous national monuments are the three that have gigantic bridges and arches of rock. All are in the lonely, almost roadless country of southeastern Utah near the famous "Four Corners." Here is a region of fantastic buttes and mesas, gullies, and deep canyons through which rivers bend in wide S-curves.

Arches National Monument is in the heart of this land. It has more natural stone arches, windows, spires, and towers than any

Along Park Avenue, Arches National Monument, Utah (National Park Service photo by L. M. Pierson)

other area in the country. So far, eighty-eight arches have been found. In addition, erosion has carved the red sandstone into many weird shapes: men, animals, buildings, and thrones. In one section, wind and water have tunneled windows into the solid rock walls. In another, a canyon lined with great towers of rock is called Park Avenue because of its likeness to one of New York City's streets of tall buildings. The longest natural stone span in the world is Landscape Arch, 291 feet long. Many other parts of the monument — Devils Garden, Klondike Bluffs, and Fiery Furnace — have not yet been fully explored.

The rock arches started to form when water entered vertical cracks that crisscross the rocks at right angles. Over the ages the minerals in the cracks dissolved, and the cracks became wide openings separating huge upright slabs of sandstone called "fins." The water, gradually eating through the thick fins, formed holes, or windows, in them. Wind and weather continually make the holes larger and smooth them into arches. In time, the arches are worn so thin that the tops collapse and only the pillars remain. New arches are forming all the time, however.

Unlike a natural arch, a natural bridge is formed by the action of a stream or river against a fin of rock. Originally rivers in this region were channeled into curving canyons. As a result they twisted and turned every few yards. A river always tries to short-cut across its curves, however. Anything that blocks its way is gradually worn down by the force of the water, and the sand and gravel it carries. In time, the river smashes an opening through weak spots in the rock that stands in its path. Then more and more water pours through the gap, widening and deepening it until the tiny hole has become a natural bridge. At the same time, the river has abandoned its former curve.

Natural Bridges National Monument has three huge sandstone bridges. Each has a Hopi Indian name, for the Hopis are the de-

The Owachomó Bridge, Natural Bridges National Monument, Utah
(National Park Service photo by George Grant)

scendants of the prehistoric people who lived in the region. The oldest bridge is Owachomó; it spans a 600-foot-deep canyon. It is 106 feet high, 180 feet long, and 9 feet thick. Sipapu is middle-aged. It is 220 feet high, 268 feet long, and 53 feet thick. The pillars of both these bridges are far enough apart so that the river waters no longer grind them away. Kachina, the youngest bridge, is still being enlarged by the river that runs under it. It is 210 feet

Rainbow Bridge, Rainbow Bridge National Monument, Utah
(National Park Service photo by Warren Hamilton)

high, 206 feet long, and 93 feet thick. As the bridges grow older they get thinner, for wind and frost continue to wear away the rock. Eventually they will get so thin that a crack will develop and grow wider, and one day the bridge will crash down.

A rainbow was changed by the gods to stone; that is what the Indians said about *Rainbow Bridge National Monument*, the third

70

and greatest of Utah's rock-span formations. Its span is thicker at the center than a three-story building is tall. It is 33 feet wide — wider than a two-lane highway. And its 309-foot-high arch is tall enough to go over the national Capitol in Washington, D. C. It is the largest natural bridge in the world.

Rainbow Bridge is hidden away in the rugged country of southern Utah, in such a lonely region that it can be reached only by a ride along a fourteen-mile horse trail, or by a six-mile hike from a Colorado River boat landing. Even the Indians who live on nearby reservations have, for the most part, never made the trip to see it. The bridge was discovered in 1909 by archaeologist Dr. Byron Cummings, who found it by tracing the Indian legends of an immense arch called Nonnozoshi. The comparatively few people who have made the journey to Rainbow Bridge are filled with wonder at the sight. The prehistoric peoples who camped near it must have felt the same way, for among the ancient ruins are religious altars.

Chiricahua National Monument, in southern Arizona, is a region of volcanic lava. As the hardened lava was tilted into cliffs and mountains, it cracked. Erosion worked along the cracks and undercut the blocks of rock to make pillars and strangely shaped pinnacles. There are many balanced rocks, and rock towers that look like piles of huge blocks put together by a giant baby. Some rocks have been ground into shapes resembling animals and people. During the wars with the Apache Indians, under their famous chiefs Cochise, Geronimo, and Massai, the Chiricahua region was the scene of violent battles.

Pinnacles National Monument, in western California, is another ancient volcanic area. Rock spires rise as much as 1,200 feet above jagged canyons, and the lava cliffs are undercut into caves and crags. The monument is known for the variety of its animal and bird life. Nearly one hundred bird species have been seen, including the rare duck hawk, prairie falcon, and golden eagle.

Punch and Judy, Chiricahua National Monument, Arizona
(National Park Service photo by George Grant)

In two national monuments the canyons that have been cut are of greater interest than the cliffs that remain. One is Arizona's *Grand Canyon National Monument,* a wild and lonely section near

Grand Canyon National Park. It has lookout points that tower over the Inner Gorge of the Colorado River. Better known is *Black Canyon of the Gunnison National Monument*, in Colorado.

**Inner Gorge, Grand Canyon National Monument, Arizona
(National Park Service photo by E. T. Scoyen)**

Black Canyon of the Gunnison National Monument, Colorado
(Bureau of Reclamation photo)

This narrow, rugged chasm carved deep between sheer-walled black cliffs is a grim spot. The dark rocks of the walls are millions of years old. The bottom of the canyon is shrouded in gloom except when the sun is overhead at midday. The gorge reaches 2,425 feet in depth, yet the cliff rims are only 1,300 feet apart in places; the river has been deepening its channel faster than erosion can widen the canyon.

Petrified Forest National Monument, in eastern Arizona, is the graveyard of an ancient forest whose fallen trees were buried by mud and sand. The earth that covered the logs contained quantities of volcanic ash, rich in a mineral called silica. The silica was dissolved by underground water, and deposited in the wood of the trees until they became entirely mineralized, or petrified. The mineral agate gave the logs brilliant colors; quartz formed beauti-

Gully filled with petrified wood, Petrified Forest National Monument, Arizona (National Park Service photo by George Grant)

Ancient writings on cliffs, Petrified Forest National Monument, Arizona
(National Park Service photo by George Grant)

ful crystals in them. Much later they were unearthed by erosion.

Now giant mineral logs and bits of petrified wood litter the sands of this unusual region. The monument was created to protect the forest from destruction by souvenir-hunters and gem-collectors who sometimes dynamited entire logs to get at the jewel-like crystals inside them. Prehistoric people must have lived in the region, for there are many ancient writings carved in rock walls. Most famous is Newspaper Rock, which is covered with the carvings.

A part of the monument is also a section of the Painted Desert, an area of cliffs eroded into fantastic shapes. It is unusual because of its many colors — red, blue, brown, and yellow — caused by minerals in the rocks. Clouds, rain, sunrise and sunset, and moonlight each bring out a different set of colors.

Different from all the other monuments is *Glacier Bay National Monument,* on the southeast coast of Alaska. Here, in an almost unexplored wilderness of towering mountains and more than twenty great glaciers, is a fifty-mile-long bay fed by melting ice.

As snow constantly piles up in the two mountain ranges that border the bay, pressure changes it to ice which forms glaciers. They are forced to move forward, like rivers of ice, down the mountain valleys toward the sea. Some move an inch a day; some move as much as 30 feet. Some actually reach the ocean; others fall short because the warmer air near the water melts their front ends, or "snouts," as fast as they move ahead. If the climate warms up, the ice melts even faster and the snouts back up even though the glaciers themselves are still flowing downhill.

The snouts of the glaciers that feed Glacier Bay have moved back and forth many times as the climate warmed and cooled. In the year 1700 almost all of Glacier Bay was covered with a layer of ice over half a mile thick. Even sixty years ago some inlets at the northern end were ice-covered. In 1899 an earthquake broke thousands of chunks of ice away from the glaciers, which melted rapidly for many years thereafter. In recent years they have continued to draw back from the bay, though at a slower rate.

Famous in the area is Muir Glacier, two miles wide, with a sheer cliff face rising 265 feet above the water. A chunk of ice breaking away from it and falling into the bay sends up 30-foot

Rendu Glacier, Glacier Bay National Monument, Alaska
(U. S. Forest Service photo)

waves. Sometimes Glacier Bay is jammed with floating icebergs. Tides are high, currents are fierce, and storms are frequent. But visitors to the national monument can walk in mossy forests, perhaps glimpse brown bears and grizzlies, and possibly see a rare, bluish glacier bear. Mountain goats climb the cliffs, porpoises and whales play in the waters, and seals sprawl on icebergs.

**Looking south at Lamplugh Glacier, Glacier Bay National Monument, Alaska
(National Park Service photo by Lowell Sumner)**

Dome Mountain, Lava Beds National Monument, California
(National Park Service photo by George Grant)

The National Park Service

The National Park Service is responsible for 25 million acres of America's scenic marvels and historic sites. In addition to the national parks and monuments, it administers

National Historical Parks,
National Military Parks,
National Memorial Parks,
National Battlefield Parks,
National Battlefield Sites,
National Memorials,
National Historic Sites,
National Cemeteries,
National Parkways,
National Capital Parks,
National Recreation Areas,
National Seashore Recreational Areas.

80

This immense task is performed by a devoted staff, headed by a director. Under his national headquarters in Washington, D.C., are five regional offices: in Richmond, Virginia; Omaha, Nebraska; Santa Fe, New Mexico; San Francisco, California; and Philadelphia, Pennsylvania. Except for the most remote ones, each national monument has a superintendent in charge. Depending on its size and location, there are one or more park rangers on duty to guide visitors and to see that they observe National Park Service rules.

Obviously every visitor would like to take home a souvenir. But if each of the millions who tour the national monuments annually were to pick up a bit of rock, or a beautiful flower, or a piece of petrified wood it would not be too many years before the monument was stripped bare. For this reason — to preserve the monument for the millions yet to come — regulations guard against souvenir-hunting. There are other common-sense rules designed to protect people, plants, and animals, and to make a visit to a national monument enjoyable for all.

Here are the basic rules common to all monuments:

1. Do not molest wild birds or animals, or pick wild flowers. Dogs and cats brought into monuments must be kept on a leash.

2. Do not pick up any souvenirs, walk on historic or prehistoric ruins, or mar ruins or canyon walls or other surfaces.

3. Camp and picnic at designated places only. Be careful with fire; campfires may be built only at designated places.

4. Hunting or shooting is prohibited.

5. Do not litter monuments with refuse.

6. When driving, observe the speed limits. Report all accidents to the nearest ranger station.

7. In Indian-inhabited monuments do not enter Indian dwellings or photograph Indians without permission.

8. Do not roll or throw rocks or other objects off cliffs or other high places.

9. Hiking and climbing alone is dangerous. Either go with the ranger guide or report to him before you start out on side trips, and tell him where you are headed.

10. Some monuments have special precautions which must be observed, and which will be posted at headquarters. (An example: Drivers are warned not to drive over the loose, shifting sands at Great Sand Dunes National Monument.)

Monuments, Listed by State

The wide-open spaces of the West have a near monopoly on national monuments. Almost all of the scenic and prehistoric monument sites lie in Arizona, California, Colorado, New Mexico, and Utah. Here is a state-by-state location guide to the national monuments:

ALABAMA
Russell Cave
  (being made ready)

ALASKA
Glacier Bay
Katmai
Sitka

ARIZONA
Canyon de Chelly
Casa Grande
Chiricahua
Grand Canyon
Montezuma Castle
Navajo
Organ Pipe Cactus
Petrified Forest
Pipe Spring
Saguaro
Sunset Crater
Tonto
Tumacacori
Tuzigoot
Walnut Canyon
Wupatki

CALIFORNIA
Cabrillo
Channel Islands
Death Valley
  (partly in Nevada)
Devils Postpile
Joshua Tree
Lava Beds
Muir Woods
Pinnacles

COLORADO
Black Canyon of the
  Gunnison
Colorado
Great Sand Dunes
Hovenweep
  (partly in Utah)
Yucca House
  (not open to the public)

FLORIDA
Castillo de San Marcos
Fort Jefferson
Fort Matanzas

GEORGIA
Fort Frederica
Fort Pulaski
Ocmulgee

IDAHO
Craters of the Moon

IOWA
Effigy Mounds

MARYLAND
Fort McHenry

MINNESOTA
Pipestone

MISSISSIPPI
Ackia Battleground

MISSOURI
George Washington
  Carver

MONTANA
Big Hole Battlefield
Custer Battlefield

NEBRASKA
Homestead
Scotts Bluff

NEVADA
Lehman Caves

NEW JERSEY
Edison Laboratory

NEW MEXICO
Aztec Ruins
Bandelier
Capulin Mountain
Chaco Canyon
El Morro
Fort Union
Gila Cliff Dwellings
Gran Quivira
White Sands

NEW YORK
Castle Clinton
Statue of Liberty

OHIO
Mound City Group
Perry's Victory and
  International Peace
  Memorial

OREGON
Oregon Caves

SOUTH CAROLINA
Fort Sumter

SOUTH DAKOTA	Cedar Breaks	WASHINGTON
Badlands	Dinosaur	Fort Vancouver
Jewel Cave	(mostly in Colorado)	Whitman
	Natural Bridges	
TENNESSEE	Rainbow Bridges	WEST VIRGINIA
Andrew Johnson	Timpanogos Cave	Harpers Ferry
Meriwether Lewis		(partly in Maryland)
	VIRGINIA	
UTAH	Booker T. Washington	WYOMING
Arches	George Washington	Devils Tower
Capitol Reef	Birthplace	Fort Laramie

**Exhibit room, Edison Laboratory National Monument, New Jersey
(Thomas Alva Edison Foundation photo)**

Post Office Addresses of Monuments

Monument name	Size in acres	Date established	For more information write to the superintendent at this address
ACKIA BATTLEGROUND	49	Oct. 25, 1938	c/o Natchez Trace Parkway, Box 428, Tupelo, Miss.
ANDREW JOHNSON	16	April 27, 1942	Greeneville, Tenn.
ARCHES	34,249	April 12, 1929	Box 98, Moab, Utah
AZTEC RUINS	27	Jan. 24, 1923	Box 457, Aztec, N.M.
BADLANDS	111,529	Jan. 25, 1939	Box 72, Interior, S.D.
BANDELIER	27,103	Feb. 11, 1916	Santa Fe, N.M.
BIG HOLE BATTLEFIELD	200	June 23, 1910	c/o Yellowstone National Park, Yellowstone Park, Wyo.
BLACK CANYON OF THE GUNNISON	14,464	March 2, 1933	Box 157, Fruita, Colo.
BOOKER T. WASHINGTON	164	June 18, 1957	c/o Blue Ridge Parkway, Box 1710, Roanoke, Va.
CABRILLO	80	Oct. 14, 1913	Box 6175, San Diego, Calif.
CANYON DE CHELLY	83,840	April 1, 1931	Box 8, Chinle, Ariz.
CAPITOL REEF	39,172	Aug. 2, 1937	Torrey, Utah
CAPULIN MOUNTAIN	680	Aug. 9, 1916	Box 94, Capulin, N.M.
CASA GRANDE	472	Aug. 3, 1918	Box 518, Coolidge, Ariz.
CASTILLO DE SAN MARCOS	19	Oct. 15, 1924	Box 1431, St. Augustine, Fla.
CASTLE CLINTON	1	July 13, 1950	c/o Statue of Liberty National Monument, Liberty Island, New York 4, N.Y.
CEDAR BREAKS	6,172	Aug. 22, 1933	c/o Zion National Park, Springdale, Utah
CHACO CANYON	21,509	Mar. 11, 1907	Bloomfield, N.M.
CHANNEL ISLANDS	26,819	April 26, 1938	Box 6175, San Diego, Calif.
CHIRICAHUA	10,645	April 18, 1924	Dos Cabezas, Ariz.
COLORADO	17,783	May 24, 1911	Box 157, Fruita, Colo.
CRATERS OF THE MOON	48,183	May 2, 1924	Box 188, Arco, Idaho

Monument name	Size in acres	Date established	For more information write to the superintendent at this address
CUSTER BATTLEFIELD	765	Mar. 22, 1946	Box 116, Crow Agency, Mont.
DEATH VALLEY	1,907,760	Feb. 11, 1933	Death Valley, Calif.
DEVILS POSTPILE	798	July 6, 1911	c/o Yosemite National Park, Box 577, Yosemite National Park, Calif.
DEVILS TOWER	1,346	Sept. 24, 1906	Devils Tower, Wyo.
DINOSAUR	209,744	Oct. 4, 1915	Box 621, Vernal, Utah
EDISON LABORATORY	1	July 14, 1956	Box 126, Orange, N.J.
EFFIGY MOUNDS	1,204	Oct. 25, 1949	Box K, McGregor, Iowa
EL MORRO	1,278	Dec. 8, 1906	El Morro, N.M.
FORT FREDERICA	250	Sept. 10, 1945	Box 367, St. Simons Island, Ga.
FORT JEFFERSON	47,125	Jan. 4, 1935	c/o Everglades National Park, Box 275, Homestead, Fla.
FORT LARAMIE	214	July 16, 1938	Fort Laramie, Wyo.
FORT MATANZAS	227	Oct. 15, 1924	Box 1431, St. Augustine, Fla.
FORT MCHENRY	43	March 3, 1925	Baltimore 30, Md.
FORT PULASKI	5,516	Oct. 15, 1924	Box 204, Savannah Beach, Ga.
FORT SUMTER	2	July 12, 1948	U.S. Custom House, Charleston, S.C.
FORT UNION	720	April 5, 1956	Watrous, N.M.
FORT VANCOUVER	90	July 9, 1954	Vancouver, Wash.
GEORGE WASHINGTON BIRTHPLACE	393	Jan. 23, 1930	Washington's Birthplace, Westmoreland County, Va.
GEORGE WASHINGTON CARVER	210	June 14, 1951	Box 726, Diamond, Mo.
GILA CLIFF DWELLINGS	160	Nov. 16, 1907	Box 679, Silver City, N.M.
GLACIER BAY	2,274,595	Feb. 26, 1925	Box 1781, Juneau, Alaska
GRAND CANYON	198,280	Dec. 22, 1932	c/o Grand Canyon National Park, Grand Canyon, Ariz.

Monument name	Size in acres	Date established	For more information write to the superintendent at this address
GRAN QUIVIRA	610	Nov. 1, 1909	Box 18, Gran Quivira, N.M.
GREAT SAND DUNES	36,740	Mar. 17, 1932	Box 60, Alamosa, Colo.
HARPERS FERRY	1,500	June 30, 1944	Box 117, Harpers Ferry, W. Va.
HOMESTEAD	162	Jan. 3, 1939	Route 1, Beatrice, Neb.
HOVENWEEP	505	March 2, 1923	c/o Mesa Verde National Park, Colo.
JEWEL CAVE	1,274	Feb. 7, 1908	c/o Wind Cave National Park, Hot Springs, S.D.
JOSHUA TREE	557,934	Aug. 10, 1936	Box 875, Twentynine Palms, Calif.
KATMAI	2,697,590	Sept. 24, 1918	c/o Mt. McKinley National Park, McKinley Park, Alaska
LAVA BEDS	46,238	Nov. 21, 1925	Box 867, Tulelake, Calif.
LEHMAN CAVES	640	Jan. 24, 1922	Baker, Nev.
MERIWETHER LEWIS	300	Feb. 6, 1925	c/o Natchez Trace Parkway, Box 428, Tupelo, Miss.
MONTEZUMA CASTLE	783	Dec. 8, 1906	Box 218, Camp Verde, Ariz.
MOUND CITY GROUP	67	March 2, 1923	Box 332, Chillicothe, Ohio
MUIR WOODS	504	Jan. 9, 1908	Mill Valley, Calif.
NATURAL BRIDGES	2,649	April 16, 1908	c/o Region Three, N.P.S., Box 1728, Santa Fe, N.M.
NAVAJO	360	March 20, 1909	Tonalea, Ariz.
OCMULGEE	683	Dec. 23, 1936	Box 936, Macon, Ga.
OREGON CAVES	480	July 12, 1909	c/o Crater Lake National Park, Crater Lake, Ore.
ORGAN PIPE CACTUS	330,874	April 13, 1937	Box 38, Ajo, Ariz.
PERRY'S VICTORY AND INTERNATIONAL PEACE MEMORIAL	14	July 6, 1936	Drawer D, Put-in-Bay, Ohio

Monument name	Size in acres	Date established	For more information write to the superintendent at this address
PETRIFIED FOREST	94,161	Dec. 8, 1906	Box 518, Holbrook, Ariz.
PINNACLES	14,497	Jan. 16, 1908	Paicines, Calif.
PIPE SPRING	40	May 31, 1923	Moccasin, Ariz.
PIPESTONE	282	Aug. 25, 1937	Pipestone, Minn.
RAINBOW BRIDGE	160	May 30, 1910	c/o Region Three, N.P.S., Box 1728, Santa Fe, N.M.
RUSSELL CAVE	(being made ready)		
SAGUARO	63,284	March 1, 1933	Route 8, Box 350, Tucson, Ariz.
SCOTTS BLUFF	3,451	Dec. 12, 1919	Box 136, Gering, Neb.
SITKA	54	March 23, 1910	Box 1781, Juneau, Alaska
STATUE OF LIBERTY	10	Oct. 15, 1924	Liberty Island New York 4, N.Y.
SUNSET CRATER	3,040	May 26, 1930	c/o Region Three, N.P.S., Box 1728, Santa Fe, N.M.
TIMPANOGOS CAVE	250	Oct. 14, 1922	R.F.D. No. 1, Box 287, American Fork, Utah
TONTO	1,120	Dec. 19, 1907	Box 1088, Roosevelt, Ariz.
TUMACACORI	10	Sept. 15, 1908	Box 6, Tumacacori, Ariz.
TUZIGOOT	42	July 25, 1939	Box 36, Clarkdale, Ariz.
WALNUT CANYON	1,879	Nov. 30, 1915	Route, 1, Box 790, Flagstaff, Ariz.
WHITE SANDS	146,535	Jan. 18, 1933	Box 231, Alamogordo, N.M.
WHITMAN	95	Jan. 20, 1940	Route 2, Walla Walla, Wash.
WUPATKI	35,693	Dec. 9, 1924	Tuba Star Route, Flagstaff, Ariz.
YUCCA HOUSE (not open to the public)	9	Dec. 19, 1919	c/o Mesa Verde National Park, Colo.

Index